The

Five Gifts

Experiencing the Divine in Everyday Life

www.the5gifts.com

The

Five Gifts

Experiencing the Divine in Everyday Life

by Joe Hahn, RYT
www.the5gifts.com

Balboa Press books may be ordered through booksellers or by contacting:

Balboa Press
A Division of Hay House
1663 Liberty Drive
Bloomington, IN 47403
www.balboapress.com
1-(877) 407-4847

Because of the dynamic nature of the Internet, any web addresses or links contained in this book may have changed since publication and may no longer be valid. The views expressed in this work are solely those of the author and do not necessarily reflect the views of the publisher, and the publisher hereby disclaims any responsibility for them.

The author of this book does not dispense medical advice or prescribe the use of any technique as a form of treatment for physical, emotional, or medical problems without the advice of a physician, either directly or indirectly. The intent of the author is only to offer information of a general nature to help you in your quest for emotional and spiritual well-being. In the event you use any of the information in this book for yourself, which is your constitutional right, the author and the publisher assume no responsibility for your actions.

Any people depicted in stock imagery provided by Thinkstock are models, and such images are being used for illustrative purposes only.
Certain stock imagery © Thinkstock.

ISBN: 978-1-4525-3352-0 (sc)
ISBN: 978-1-4525-3353-7 (e)

Library of Congress Control Number: 2011903988

Printed in the United States of America

Balboa Press rev. date: 03/23/2011

BALBOA
PRESS
A DIVISION OF HAY HOUSE

to
Cathy
with
love

Acknowledgements

I am deeply grateful to all of my teachers, and to everyone who helped an encouraged me as I wrote this book. A very special thanks to Marian Worthington for her wonderful assistance in proof-reading the final draft. Additional thanks to Marian, and to Rev. Henry Simoni-Wastilla, Linda Simoni-Wastilla, Betty Hahn, Bill Hahn, Cathy Clark, Liz Clark, and Alice Reid for reading and commenting on an early draft of this book. Your input and encouragement was invaluable. Special thanks to Alice Reid for your wonderful spiritual counseling, and to Cathy Kosinski for being a willing sounding board for many ideas.

My love to you all. Namaste.

Table of Contents

PROLOGUE: SHARING THOUGHTS

I will be sharing a few thoughts with you in the pages that follow. As you read, you will agree with some of these thoughts, but not all. There will be an impulse for you to share your thoughts, and if we were together, we would compare thoughts. You would say what you think, and I would say what I think about what you think, and so on. If we agree in our thinking, we would create a pleasant ego boost for each other. If we disagree, our egos would clash in unpleasant conflict.

Whether we agree or disagree, I do not want to go with you into the place of 'I think.' Rather, I invite you to go with me to a place of 'I am.' 'I am' is an opening to awareness beyond the limits of thought. In this new, expanded awareness, we can each be aware of the thoughts that enter into our minds, and recognize that the gift of thought is a useful tool, and, at the same time, a limited one.

From this place of expanded awareness, we can each observe in two directions - let's call these directions *inward* and *outward.* Our observations engender two key understandings. It is difficult to describe our observations and understandings, because words are tools of thought, and we are observing from awareness beyond the limits of thought. Any description we use will be self-limiting. Nevertheless, I will try.

Looking inward, we see the manifest world as we know it. We observe the thoughts that pass through the mind-space, the experiences we have in our lives, and all that we sense and do with our physical bodies. Looking inward, we realize that this manifest world is all that we see most of the time, and our awareness is dominated by 'I think'. Most significantly, we realize that what 'I think' isn't all that important.

2

Looking outward offers a more profound understanding. When we *turn the camera around* from what we focus on most of the time, we catch a glimpse of the divine source. This is the source of 'I am.' It is the infinite, unmanifest source of all that is manifest. Beyond words, beyond thought, beyond our capacity to comprehend, the divine is the source of all the gifts we receive. When we open to the source, we come to know that *each of us is a unique and beautiful manifestation of the divine source, and we all share the same divine light.*

This knowing is called *awakening.*

We are all invited to awaken. In the past, only a small number of individuals were capable of expanded awareness. We called them sages, saints, avatars. Today, this awareness is available to everyone. All of humanity is awakening to oneness. Of course, some will choose to remain asleep. Some will resist the shift in awareness. That's sad. But, it is not so important, for, when the water level rises, all the boats float higher.

The water level is rising. The awakening of humanity is underway. You and I are invited.

The ideas in this book are designed to move you along your path of awakening. My intent is to help you know the truth: that all we have is a gift from the divine, that each of us is an expression of divine grace, and that we are one in the divine light. Please enjoy these gifts.

Namaste
Joe

OVERVIEW OF THE FIVE GIFTS

I am a hole
in the flute
through which the
Christ's breath
flows.
Listen to
this music.
~Hafiz

Being here is a gift. All that we have, all that we are, each of us is a gift from a divine source. Yet, most of us forget the wonder of the gifts we've received, most of the time. Our forgetfulness does not diminish the gifts in any way. We simply lose access to the power of the source from which these gifts come.

This book is a gift. The concepts in this book were given to me in a brilliant flash of insight, from a source beyond my comprehension. With this insight also came a compulsion to share these ideas with others. This book is about remembering, and in our remembering, we reconnect to the spirit of the universe that gives us the gifts we receive.

Taken together, *the five gifts* is a model for understanding ourselves and each other. Each gift describes an essential facet of our being, as we exist in this human form. The five gifts are:

- ◇ The gift of the physical body
- ◇ The gift of life
- ◇ The gift of thought
- ◇ The gift of awareness, and
- ◇ The gift of divine grace.

Each gift is an expression of the divine source, which is consciousness itself. We are given these gifts, as each of us is an act of divine creation.

The Five Gifts and The Ancient Wisdom of India: The Maya Koshas

Over the last couple of years, I've been exploring and teaching the insights of the five gifts. I've found it helpful to explain the five gifts in the context of other wisdom sources. The first of these sources is ancient wisdom from India, where yoga originates. The *Taittiriya Upanishad* (2), one of the spiritual texts of India, tells us that there are five *maya koshas*. The Sanskrit word *kosha* means shell, or layer, analogous to the peel of an orange. *Maya* implies existence, or living in this world. Each of the *maya koshas* is a description of a layer or component shell of our human existence. The *maya koshas* are:

- *Ana Maya Kosha* - the "food shell," or physical layer of the body
- *Prana Maya Kosha* - the layer of subtle life energy
- *Mano Maya Kosha* - the mind layer
- *Vishnana Maya Kosha* - the layer of understanding, and
- *Ananda Maya Kosha* - the shell of bliss.

As you can see, the *maya koshas* correlate quite closely to the five gifts. The *koshas* also roughly match what we in the west would describe as parts of ourselves, namely: mind, body, heart and spirit. Most useful to our exploration is the

The Five Gifts as Koshas

1. *Ana maya kosha* – the gift of the physical body

2. *Prana maya kosha* – the gift of life

3. *Mano maya kosha* – the gift of thought

4. *Vishnana maya kosha* - the gift of awareness

5. *Ananda maya kosha* - the gift of divine grace

7

koshas as a description of overlapping shells, with each shell encompassing and expanding beyond the ones it contains. Each of the *koshas* is a layer, which exists within the subsequent layers. *Ana maya kosha* exists within *prana maya kosha*, which in turn exists within *mano maya kosha*, and so on.

This same hierarchical relationship holds within the five gifts. As the graphic on the previous page shows:

> the gift of the physical body is contained within and permeated by
> the gift of life, which expands beyond the limits of the body, and is, in turn, surrounded and permeated by
> the gift of thought, more expansive than either the body or the life energy field, yet contained within
> the gift of awareness. All of these gifts come from and are contained within the infinite source, which we will call
> the gift of divine grace.

As we discuss the hierarchical relationship between the gifts, we need to be clear about what a hierarchy is. As Ken Wilber (3) describes so eloquently, there are two types of hierarchies: oppressive hierarchies, and growth hierarchies. The hierarchy we observe within the five gifts is a growth hierarchy. The intent of the five gifts is to facilitate our growth in awareness.

Let me restate. The intention of these gifts, which come to us from a divine source, is to support our growth. As we grow in awareness, we experience greater joy and love.

My intention, too, in writing this book, is to help you grow in awareness, and to expand your joyful life experience.

8

The Five Gifts and
The Map of Consciousness

Another way for us to understand the five gifts is to draw upon the work of contemporary spiritual teacher, Dr. David Hawkins, MD, PhD. In his book, *Power vs. Force* (4), Dr. Hawkins describes a Map of Consciousness. The map is a continuum, a logarithmic scale from 0 to 1,000, describing the scope of human consciousness. The numbers were chosen for convenience; the actual values are not important. There are, however, two key understandings for our discussion of the five gifts that come from the work of Dr. Hawkins.

First, the scale of the Map of Consciousness is logarithmic, and the energy grows exponentially as awareness expands to higher levels on the map. This means that, for example, a calibration of 201 on the map is not merely one greater than 200, but an order of magnitude greater. Small movements up or down the map represent great leaps in conscious awareness.

The second key understanding from the Map of Consciousness is that consciousness is expressed within a discreet range for each of the five gifts, and for human awareness itself. It may be obvious to us that the human body has limitations, but the Map of Consciousness also tells us that, while we are anchored in this human form, our awareness has limits as well. Or, as Alice Reid, my good friend and spiritual teacher would say, "as long as we have skin," we have limits.

We can use kinesiology to calibrate each of *the five gifts* on the Map of Consciousness. The graphic on the next page shows the calibrations I have done. Each of the gifts has a calibration range, as follows:
- ➢ the gift of the physical body, 0 to 99

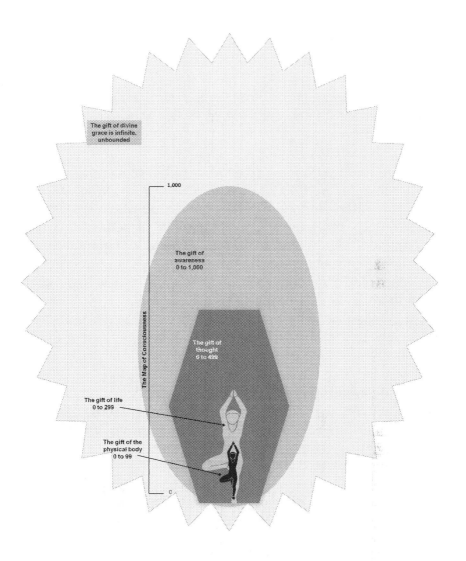

The gift of divine grace is infinite, unbounded

1,000

The gift of awareness 0 to 1,000

The Map of Consciousness

The gift of thought 0 to 499

The gift of life 0 to 299

The gift of the physical body 0 to 99

0

Calibration of *The Five Gifts*
on
The Map of Consciousness (2)

> the gift of life, 0 to 299
> the gift of thought, 0 to 499
> the gift of awareness, 0 to 1,000.

The gift of divine grace does not calibrate on the Map of Consciousness, since this gift is un-measurable, unlimited and unbounded.

Our calibration of the five gifts on the Map of Consciousness re-affirms what we know from the ancient wisdom of the *koshas*, that each of the five gifts is contained within the others. What's more, the Map of Consciousness introduces the idea of direction along a continuum. The continuum of consciousness (quantified for human beings by Dr. Hawkins with the Map of Consciousness) is an exponentially expanding phenomenon, and a property of the universe. Our piece of consciousness is rather small, yet, for us, it is significant. As we move "up" in our exploration, we encounter higher levels of awareness within the continuum.

This directional nature of the map of consciousness is useful. However, we must be cautious. Using words like "up" and "higher" in western culture often denote value judgments. Up is usually considered better; higher consciousness is thought to be superior. We must resist such value judgments. "Up" and "higher" are directions only. While we may find ourselves drawn to higher states of awareness, this does not make us superior.

Keeping this caution in mind, we can learn from an application of the Map of Consciousness to our exploration of the five gifts. Moving up the map of consciousness, we observe the following trends.

> **Limited to expansive** - As we move up the continuum, we find that each gift expands beyond the limits of the

previous ones. The gift of the physical body is the most limited of the five gifts. The gift of life is a field of energy that permeates and animates the physical body - and expands beyond the limits of the body. The gift of thought is more expansive, and so on. The gift of divine grace is limitless.

➢ **Density to subtlety** - The physical body is the most dense of the the five gifts, and moving up the continuum, each gift becomes more subtle. The gift of life, which is often referred to as "the subtle body", is more subtle than physical matter, thought is more subtle than life, and awareness more subtle than thought. The gift of divine grace is without form or structure.

➢ **Expanding Energy and Power** - Moving up the continuum, we also find a progression of increasing energy and power. The lowest energy is the most dense - the physical body. The gift of life expands energetically beyond the limits of the body. The gift of divine grace is an unlimited source of power and energy - the source of all that is.

Understanding the Each of Five Gifts

In the coming chapters, we will explore each of the five gifts individually. As we do, we will use six keys to help us understand these gifts. The keys are:

➢ **Expression of Consciousness** – Consciousness is a property of the universe, and each of the five gifts is a unique expression of consciousness.

➢ **Kosha** – We will draw upon the wisdom of ancient India to shed light on each of these gifts.

➢ **Level of Consciousness** – Using kinesiology, we will calibrate each gift on Dr. David Hawkins' map of consciousness.

➢ **Intention** – The universe is a field of intention. There is a reason we have received each of these gifts.

➢ **Manifestation of dis-ease** – Within each gift, we have a marker for dis-ease.

➢ **Key to wellness** – And, each gift has a key to wellness, which we will explore.

CHAPTER 1
THE GIFT OF THE
PHYSICAL BODY

*"We shape clay into a pot,
but it is the
emptiness inside
that holds
whatever we want.*

*We hammer wood
for a house,
but it is the
inner space
that makes
it livable."*
- Lao-tsu

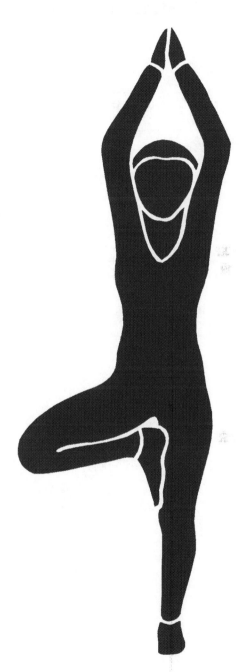

The Gift of the Physical Body

Summary

Consciousness expressed as	Structures
Kosha	Ana Maya Kosha – the food layer
Level of Consciousness	0 to 99
Intention	Anchor awareness Doing, taking action
Manifestation of dis-ease	Pain
Key to wellness	Alignment

This physical body is a gift of divine love, and I am grateful and honored to receive it. It is through the gift of the physical body that I am able to interact with the incredible wonder and beauty of the world around me.

In the ancient tradition of India, this first gift is called *Ana Maya Kosha*, or "the food layer". The ancient teachers understood that the physical "stuff" that makes up our physical body is the same stuff that makes up the food we eat. In modern physics, we call it matter. The physical body is composed of molecules and atoms of the same physical matter as the world around us.

On Dr. David Hawkins' map of consciousness the gift of the physical body calibrates between 0 and 99, with the scale of human consciousness ranging from 0 to 1,000. The physical body is the lowest energy, and most dense of the five gifts.

The physical body is a gift of consciousness, and consciousness is expressed in this gift as structures. We can observe these structures on several levels. The first is the macro structures of the body - the skeleton, the muscles and connective tissues, the arrangement of the organs into functional structures, the structure of the nervous system, the structure of the circulatory system, and so on. These macro structures have been studied extensively by medical scientists, and our western understanding of the body allows us to be aware of the elegance and wonder of the physical body.

A closer observation of this gift reveals a set of deeper structures. The cellular structures of the physical body are more than just the arrangement of building blocks. Each cell has an internal structure that allows it to function in a unique and powerful way. Each cell has, in other words, its own *Ana Maya Kosha*, or physical body. The structures of the cell

Structures of the Gift of the Physical Body

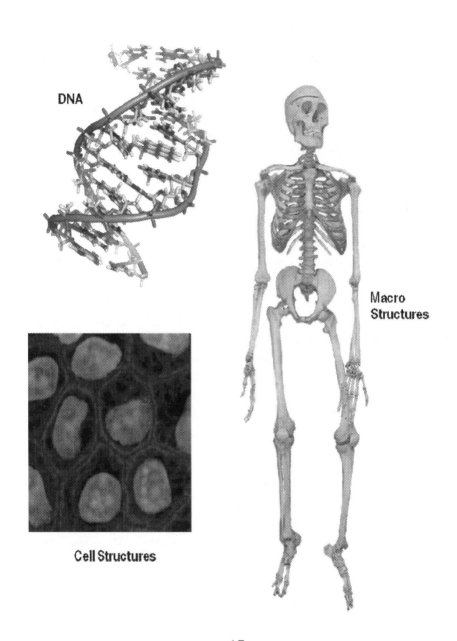

DNA

Macro
Structures

Cell Structures

bodies are equal in elegance and wonder to the structures of our physical body.

Going deeper, we can observe the structures of the atoms and molecules of the physical body. Here we discover an astounding truth. Chemists tell us that our physical bodies are made up of the same atoms as the rocks, trees, air and water around us, and in roughly the same proportions. Our bodies are composed of carbon, hydrogen, oxygen, nitrogen, iron, sodium, and so on. The only difference between the molecules in our bodies and those in the trees are the *structures* - the arrangements of the atoms. As the ancients understood, we are made of the same stuff as the world around us. Only the structures are different.

The most profound example of consciousness expressed as structures is found in the DNA molecule. In the simplest terms, DNA is nothing more than four atoms - carbon, hydrogen, oxygen and nitrogen - arranged in a complex structure. The atoms themselves are quite common, found in billions of other molecules. The uniqueness of DNA is found in the arrangement of the atoms.

The structure of the DNA is like set of blueprints. It contains the design and instructions for the gift of physical body. It is here, in the structure of the DNA, that we can observe consciousness most elegantly expressed as structure.

INTENTION AND THE GIFT OF THE PHYSICAL BODY

The universe is a field of intention, and we are given the five gifts, each for a purpose. The intent of the physical body is two-fold.

First, the physical body serves as the anchor for our awareness. Our awareness needs to be anchored in this physical world, for us to have the fullness of our life experience, and the physical body serves this need.

What's more, the gift of the physical body is given to us to take action in the world. It is with the body that we *do* things. It is only through the body that we can act in, and interact with the world around us. Simply put, the intention of this gift is for "doing".

How we treat the body, and how we use it - these are up to us. The structures of the physical body are an expression of consciousness, yet these structures do not have awareness enough to know if we are doing good works, or not. We must, with awareness, guide our use of the body. We are each responsible for choosing how we treat and use this gift.

WELLNESS AND THE GIFT OF THE PHYSICAL BODY

Wellness comes from alignment with conscious expression, and in the gift of the physical body, consciousness is expressed as structure. When we align with the structures of the physical body, we are honoring this gift, and allowing us to experience it fully. Wellness in the physical body is achieved in three key ways:

➤ Alignment of the major structures of the body in movement and activity. The physical body is designed for movement. We can see this in the structure of the bones and joints, the muscles and connective tissue. As we move, we can choose to bring awareness to the physical structures of the body, and move as we are designed to move. The principles we learn in the practice of yoga *asana* are especially useful in building our awareness and ensuring we move with healthy alignment.

➤ Enhancing cellular health. The cell structures of the physical body are essential to our overall wellness. We enhance the health of our cells by living in an environment that keeps the cells healthy. This means breathing fresh, clean air, drinking clean, pure water and surrounding our cells with an inner environment that is clean and fresh.

➤ Building healthy molecules. The physical body is called *ana maya kosha*, which means the "layer of food". The food we eat provides the "building blocks" for the molecules of the body, including DNA. All of the body's molecules are in a continuous state of regeneration, and we need to provide a constant supply of the atoms these structures require. Eating a natural, well-balanced diet of food that is free from chemicals or impurities is essential to wellness in the physical body.

When we are misaligned, we suffer in the physical body. Pain and discomfort are the body's signals that something is amiss. When we consciously align the physical body, we experience pleasure and comfort - the body feels good.

CELEBRATING AND HONORING THE PHYSICAL BODY

Let's celebrate the gift of the physical body. Here's an invocation I use each day.

*This physical body is a gift of divine love
and I am grateful and honored to receive it.*

*I commit this day:
    To strengthen and nurture this body-gift, and
    To align these structures with awareness.*

I offer this body to divine service

I awaken to the divine source of all that is the physical universe.

Divine spirit, make of me an open channel of love and grace, and let divine grace flow through me into this world.

Use me this day to create a sacred experience for all that I encounter.

Namaste

SPECIAL SECTION 1 - CONSCIOUSNESS AND AWARENESS

In many spiritual teachings the words "consciousness" and "awareness" are treated as synonymous. In this book, I use these words differently, and they have important, unique shades of meaning.

Remember that words are tools of thought, and the meaning we give to words serves only to help with understanding. I am not trying to re-define words; nor will I try to make a case that my definitions or word usages are the right ones. I simply ask, as you read this book, that you keep in mind the meanings I'm using, which may be different from other teachers.

Consciousness is the word I use to describe the divine property of the universe. The easiest way to define consciousness is as follows: consciousness is. Consciousness exists. Consciousness is a property of the universe. What's more, consciousness is the source of everything else in the universe, including us.

You could substitute many other words for divine consciousness - God, Yahweh, Allah, Ram, the Tao, and so on. Once again, the words we use are less important than the understanding they point to. Consciousness is a relatively neutral word - it does not carry with it the trappings of any particular spiritual tradition. That's why I use it. We can interpret it in whatever way is useful to each of us.

Consciousness is the source of the universe, and the driving force behind all that happens. It is consciousness that is propelling us forward on an evolutionary path; it is consciousness that is the source of divine grace and love. It is

22

the unbounded field, the unlimited power of the whole universe.

All things are an expression of consciousness, and everything has consciousness in it. A stone has the same consciousness as an antelope, or a human being, or a star system. Consciousness is undifferentiated, and permeates all that is.

All things do not, however, *experience* consciousness equally. The awareness of a rock is not equivalent to the awareness of a child, for example. Awareness, as I use the word, describes how the objects and beings in the manifest world experience consciousness. Physical matter is conscious, but its awareness is limited to the physical structures. Plants and many animals are also limited in awareness, experiencing only life energy awareness. Rocks, plants, fish, and people all have consciousness (by my definition) since all are part of this conscious universe. However, a fish has greater awareness than a rock (so it seems), and people have greater awareness than rocks, plants or animals.

We can look at Dr. Hawkin's map of consciousness as both a description of consciousness itself - the continuum - and a map of awareness. Using kinesiology, Dr. Hawkins has calibrated the level of awareness of many things - people, objects, cultures, nations, and so on. Divine consciousness can't be calibrated - consciousness exists equally in all things. However, awareness - the capacity for experiencing consciousness - varies greatly.

Of course, awareness is more complex than a simple calibrated point on a scale. Human awareness, especially, is complex and variable. Our level of awareness changes with time and with circumstances. Nevertheless, each of us has a "center of awareness" - a level of awareness that is the "average" of our conscious experience. This is what is calibrated on the map of consciousness.

Consciousness is both the source of awareness, and the driving force for expanded awareness. Each of us is called to evolve and grow, and to raise our "center of awareness." Throughout history, human awareness has evolved, and most modern nations are now "thought-aware." This means that modern cultures have an awareness centered in the gift of thought.

Human awareness continues to evolve and expand. As I write this, there is a world-wide shift underway. More and more individuals are becoming aware of the limits of thought-centered awareness. We are learning to transcend these limits, as people, communities, and the whole of humanity grows in awareness.

Chapter 2
THE GIFT OF LIFE

*"My limbs are made glorious
by this life-throb
of ages
dancing in my
blood this moment."*
- Tagore

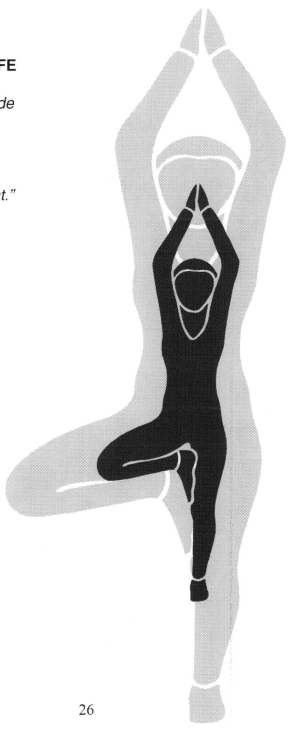

26

The Gift of Life

Summary

Consciousness expressed as	Motion and emotion
Kosha	Prana Maya Kosha – the life energy layer
Level of Consciousness	0 to 299
Intention	Experiencing
Manifestation of dis-ease	Strain, blocked energy flow
Key to wellness	Flow Happiness

Life is a gift of divine love, and I am grateful and honored to receive it. Through this gift of life I am able to move and breathe and experience the flow of divine grace.

In the ancient tradition of India, this second gift is called *Prana Maya Kosha*, or "the life energy layer". This kosha is a moving flowing energy system. It is this *prana*, or life energy that animates our physical bodies and those of all living creatures. While the substances that comprise the physical body are the same as the physical world around us, the gift of life is the difference between the rocks, dirt and air and the living world. This gift of life is one that we share with all living things.

On Dr. David Hawkins' map of consciousness, the gift of life calibrates between 0 and 299. This gift surrounds and permeates the gift of the physical body, animating our experience. The life energy field also extends beyond the limits of the physical body in both size and conscious energy.

Consciousness expresses itself in the gift of life as movement, flow and breath. We experience this gift in motion and emotion, in the flowing energy system of the physical body, in the breath, and in the movements of the cells and inner processes of the body. All living creatures also experience this gift of life as an impulse for survival, and the survival processes in us are expressed as emotions that flow through this energy field.

In many non-western healing traditions, this gift is described as *the subtle body*. The energy system of the body has a subtle structure, one that supports the living processes of the body. This subtle structure has been described in many ways, including:

➢ The Chakras and nadis of *Ayurveda*, the ancient healing art of India. These are energy centers and channels for the flow of *prana*, or life energy in the body.

➢ The meridians of Acupuncture, the ancient healing art of China. The meridians are energy pathways for the flow of *qi* (pronounced "chee"), which is life energy, analogous to *prana* of ancient India.

The Chakras

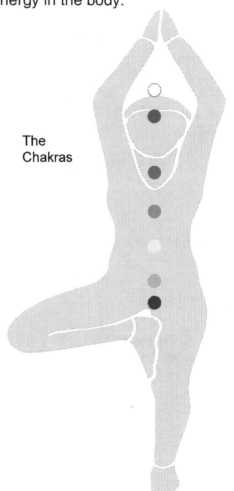

➢ The *Hun-yin* of Reiki and the practice of Shiatzu, both from the Japanese tradition. In Japanese, *ki* is the same as *qi* in Chinese and *prana* in Sanskrit.

➢ The practice of Reflexology, which has its origins in ancient Egypt, and uses the same meridian system as Chinese medicine.

➢ The Anatomy Trains (8) as described by Thomas Myers, which describes the meridians of kinetic energy throughout the physical body.

➢ Various shamanistic and native healing practices from many parts of the world, which see beyond the dense physical body and recognize the *light body* as an energy

29

field of consciousness within and around the physical structures.

The key to understanding the gift of life is to realize that energy and movement are inseparable - where there is energy there is movement, and where there is movement, there is energy. It is the gift of life that animates and moves the body; life is the energy field, the source of movement. The chakras, meridians and other subtle structures are the pathways that life energy moves through and within the body, empowering the processes and changes that are essential for us to be alive.

All that is alive shares with us this gift of life. It is life itself that provides the impulse to be alive, the impulse to survive. In our four-legged friends, this impulse for survival is expressed as instinct. Most animal behavior is driven by instinct, by the survival impulse. In humans, the survival impulse is more complex and subtle, expressed as emotions. Our emotions exist within the field of life energy, and affect motion and the life processes of the body. Emotion is life expressing itself.

INTENTION AND THE GIFT OF LIFE

There is intention behind everything that happens, and we are given the gift of life for a reason. The intent of this gift is so that we may experience the world around us. Without this life energy, we would be like the rocks and sand, inanimate, and unable to move or interact and experience anything. What's more, our emotions, which exist within the living energy field of the body, and are a manifestation of the gift of life, are what gives our life its flavor. Our emotions define our experience.

Simply put, we are intended to experience our lives.

WELLNESS AND THE GIFT OF LIFE

Without the gift of life, our physical bodies would be nothing more than clumps of chemicals, without movement or feeling. It is life that energizes these bodies. Being alive allows us to experience motion, emotion, and the stunning beauty of life around us. A healthy life energy system flows freely and naturally, and is stimulating and energetic. A lack of wellness occurs when the energy flow is blocked, unable to move.

Wellness in this gift is found in movement, motion, flow and breath. Energy must move. If life energy ceases to flow, it ceases to be. Wellness in the life energy system is achieved as follows:

➢ Movement of the breath - the breath is called *prana* in the ancient yoga tradition, which is synonymous with life energy. In the west, we think of the breath in terms of the oxygen content and other physical properties. Yet, the breath is much more - the breath is the source of life for the body. Moving the breath moves the life energy. Healthy breath is essential to a healthy life.

➢ Movement of the physical body - our bodies are designed for movement, with joints, muscles and structures that are shaped and aligned to move in powerful and useful ways. Healthy body movement is essential for wellness of the life energy system. The practices of yoga (from India) and Qigong (from China) are movement approaches that align the physical body with the breath and the life energy system. These practices are essential for our overall well-being.

➢ Emotional awareness and expression - emotion is an expression of consciousness within the gift of life, and emotional awareness is key to wellness of the life energy system. We experience emotions within the body. Yet, emotions are part of the life energy system that permeates and animates the physical body. Emotion is the interpretation we give to signals and awareness of life within the body, and the living response to our perceptions. Emotional expression does not mean that emotions run our whole life; nor is it a suppression of emotion. Rather, emotional awareness is allowing for healthy emotional responses to emerge and to teach us, and using this understanding to enhance our life experience.

➤ Creating a healthy energy environment - we are designed to live in an energy field, which surrounds and nurtures the life energy system of the body. The energy environment we live in is as important to our wellness as the physical environment. We are part of this earth where we live, and the energy of the earth - magnetism, light, heat, infrared radiation and negative ionic energy - all are essential to our wellness. Unfortunately for most of us, we spend our time in buildings that block the natural energy, or create artificial energy fields that don't match what we need for well-being. In eastern cultures, many chronic conditions are recognized as energy-deficiencies, and wellness can be restored by restoring the natural energy environment we need.

➤ Healthy sleep - the life energy system regenerates and rebalances during sleep, and lack of sleep causes great strain in this gift. Calm, restful sleep is essential. Also, sleeping in a natural energy environment - with magnetic and infrared energy at the level our energy systems need - promotes a healthier inner energy system.

➤ Living water, living food - water is the medium through which life energy moves in the body, and living water is essential to the well-being of our life. Water that has been stagnant, stored for long periods (more than a day or two) in plastic bottles, or transported over long distances through pipes needs to be reenergized to resonate with the life energy system. Water comes from a living source - the earth - and must contain the life energy to support our wellness. Food also comes from living sources, and healthy food has within it the living energy of its source. Highly processed and packaged foods are devoid of living energy and don't sustain life. Organically grown and consciously processed foods contain life energy, and promote well-being in us.

CELEBRATING AND HONORING THE GIFT OF LIFE

Let's celebrate the gift of the life. Here's an invocation I use each day.

This life is a gift of divine love
and I am grateful and honored to receive it.

I commit this day:
> *To strengthen and nurture this life-gift, and*
> *To energize this life experience with awareness*

I offer this life to divine service

I awaken to the divine spirit of life

Divine spirit, make of me an open channel of love and grace, and let divine grace flow through me into this world.

Use me this day to create a sacred experience for all that I encounter.

Namaste

Chapter 3
THE GIFT OF THOUGHT

*"The mind does not exist
within the physical body…
the body exists
within the mind"
- Deepak Chopra*

The Gift of Thought

Summary

Consciousness expressed as	Thought energy
Kosha	Mano Maya Kosha – the mind layer
Level of Consciousness	0 to 499
Intention	The 4 Ds of Thought
Manifestation of dis-ease	Stress
Key to wellness	Peace of mind Contentment

Thought is a gift of divine love, and I am grateful and honored to receive it. Through this gift of thought we are able to discern, comprehend and describe our life experience. Our thoughts come from a divine source into our minds.

In the ancient tradition of India, this third gift is called *Mano Maya Kosha*, the *living mind*. The mind is the space within which thought arises. This *kosha* surrounds, permeates and expands beyond the other layers we've discusses so far - the physical body and the life energy system. Thought comes into this mind-space and into our awareness.

Using Dr. David Hawkin's model, we calibrate the gift of thought in the range of 0 to 499. Thought permeates, learns from and guides the physical body, and the life energy field. And thought expands in conscious energy beyond either of these other gifts.

INTENTION AND THE GIFT OF THOUGHT

The gift of thought is a very powerful and wonderful gift. We are given this gift to make use of it, to understand our world and our experience. The gift of thought has four functions, which I call the four "Ds" of thought.

These are:

> Discernment - the universe has no separations, yet it is useful to discern the difference between objects and events in our experience. Thought inserts the boundaries that allow us to discern. For example, if I wish to sit on a chair, it is helpful to discern the difference between the chair, the table and the floor. Modern science and ancient wisdom both teach us that there is no real boundary, yet my ability to discern one is helpful. Even the

simplest acts, such as walking, sitting, picking up a book, and so on, would be impossible without discernment.

> Description - it is through the gift of thought that I am able to describe what I discern. Language is a tool of thought that is empowered by this gift. Using the same example as above, I can discern a difference between the table and the chair, and I can use language to describe this difference. One word is used for "table" and another or "chair". The word does not define the thing - there is no separation between the table and the chair except for the one created by the discerning thought - but the description is useful. What's more, I can describe my experience sitting on the chair and working at the table.

> Design - thought allows me to create, in my imagination, a description of something that does not exist. To continue with the above example, I can design a chair or a table. Using thought, I am able to create an image in the mind of a table just like the one I discern in the world around me, or perhaps one very different. Using thought, I can draw this mind-table, describe it to others with language, and even use my skills to build it. It starts with a design-thought.

> Decide - with the gift of thought, we receive the capacity to choose. I can discern different options, describe them to myself and others, even design new options, and select the one I wish. The selection process involves decision. Thought is the source of free will, of choice, of volition.

CHALLENGES OF THOUGHT

Many contemporary spiritual teachers tell us that our thoughts are problematic, and that spiritual growth lies in transcend-

ing thought and experiencing a more enlightened awareness. Eckhardt Tolle says, "inherent in the structure of the
human mind is a dysfunction."(4) And Albert Einstein, one of
the greatest thinkers of the past century, said "we cannot
solve today's problems using the same thinking we used to
create them." In other words, thought is the source of problems, as well as the possible solution.

I believe this thought-as-the-root-of-all-problems idea needs
to be addressed. Clearly, the gift of thought creates challenges for us. How can that be, though? How can a gift
from the divine source be problematic?

The answer lies not in the gift itself, but in what we do with it.
Thought is a tool of awareness, given us to use in a certain
way. If someone were to give you a hammer, and you used it
to drive a nail to fasten two boards together, that would be
appropriate use of the tool. However, if you use the hammer
to break a window, that is not appropriate. The problem is
not the gift, but the use. So it is with the gift of thought. Just
as there are many ways to misuse a hammer, there are
many ways to misuse thought.

Misuse of the gift of thought is a leading source of human
misery and suffering. This has been a core message of the
great spiritual teachers throughout history. Yet, most of us
are unaware of how we use - and misuse – the gift of
thought. What follows is a simple explanation that can help
us raise our awareness of our own thinking, and the errors
we make with this gift.

The first error is that we use thought to *define* things. In
doing so, we forget what thought can do, and what it cannot
do. Earlier, we talked about discernment and description,
both of which are powerful thought uses. In discernment, we
use thought to create boundaries between objects and

events in our reality. We know, from both modern science and ancient wisdom, that these boundaries are not really there, but it is useful to create them with our thoughts. With these thought-based separations, we can describe objects and events. The example we used above was the difference between a chair and a table. Through discernment, we can choose to sit on the chair and put our book on the table.

The difficulty arises when we forget that the boundaries themselves are products of thought, and instead view the separations as real. When we use thought to *define* the table and chair, we give these objects an identity and disconnection that isn't there.

Defining objects around us is a common and minor thought error. Inanimate objects can not be injured by our thinking. A more significant error, and one with greater consequences, arises when we define other people. To the discerning mind, other people appear as objects in space, separate and distinct. The mind can describe people, giving them names, and describing their physical characteristics, activities, personalities, and so on. All of this is useful discernment. The gift of thought enhances our ability to interact with one another on a day-to-day basis.

Yet, it is easy to forget that we are not really separate from each other. All great spiritual traditions share this understanding: there is one divine source from which we all emerge, and we all share the same divine light. When we define another person with our thoughts, we forget the fundamental oneness of all people. Through definition, we allow what should be a useful thought process to take on a reality and solidity that is unwarranted - even harmful. For, when another person is separate from me, I treat that other person as an object. Human history is filled with people defining and mistreating each other. It is a short step from discernment to definition, and an easy error to make. The consequences can be horrendous.

Self-definition is also an error we make with thought. When we define ourselves with thought, we forget who we really are – a divine manifestation. The mind takes over and says, "I am a father," "I am smart," "I am the president of my company," "I am overweight," and so on. None of these labels is a reflection of the truth, for any word or thought that we use puts boundaries around the truth. To say "I would be healthier if I lose some weight" can be true, because it does not define you. But to say, "I am overweight" defines you. It is not true. Some of the definitions we adopt come from others. Our culture is obsessed with labeling and defining people. Other definitions we create for ourselves. Regardless of where the label comes from, it is untrue. Let go of it.

Another error we make with thought is to take the short step from description to judgment. Description is neutral - this item is yellow, this one is blue, and so on. When we judge, however, we place a value on what we discern and describe with thought. Judgment is not neutral - this item is good because it is blue, this one is bad because it is yellow.

Judgment arises from the survival mechanisms we have as living organisms. To survive, we need to judge whether something is safe or not. When driving a car, for example, we need to judge the safety of our own actions and the actions of other drivers, and respond based on this judgment. Safety requires us to judge.

Problems arise, however, when we allow ourselves to judge beyond safety concerns. Such judgment is a misuse of the gift of thought. A tornado may be unsafe. To call it evil is an error in judgment.

Judgment errors are especially pernicious when we judge other people, or ourselves. This error in thought-use has lead to all the wars and murders and genocides and horrors that humans have perpetrated against each other throughout history. In the 20th century, humanity's judgments led to over 100 million people dying at the hands of other people. We all know the horrors that one person can commit against another. We also need to know that these horrors have at their source the misuse of the gift of thought.

So, how do we end the pattern of definition and judgment, and so end the disasters these thought patterns cause? Through expanded awareness. By becoming aware of the thoughts that enter the mind-space, and how we use thought, we can avoid the problems of misuse. We'll talk about expanded awareness in the next chapter of this book
.

MIND, BRAIN AND EGO

In the west, there has been extensive study on the function and structure of the brain, the workings of the mind, and the

expression of the ego. Many scientists, philosophers and spiritual teachers treat these three - mind, brain and ego - as synonymous. I find it useful, however, to make distinctions between these concepts, to help us better understand ourselves and the gifts we've received.

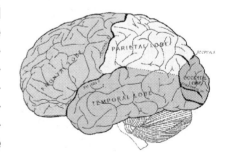

As we said earlier, the mind is the field within which thought occurs. It is like the sky, and thoughts are the clouds that pass across the sky. Some thoughts linger for a while, others are fleeting. The mind itself is simply the space for thought to exist. We can think of the mind as the potential for thought – our capacity to receive the gift of thought.

The brain is a physical organ, part of the physical body, and the physical anchor for thought. The human brain is a complex organ, and scientists have identified various parts of the brain that perform key functions within the body. Most of the inner-most parts of the brain are central controls for the physical, survival and emotional reactions within the body. It is in the outer parts of the brain – the cerebral cortex – that the gift of thought finds a physical anchor. It is here that we can see the physical manifestations of thought.

It would be a mistake, however, to equate the mind with the cerebral cortex, or any other parts of the brain. The mind cannot exist without the brain, yet the mind expands far beyond the limits of the brain. Essentially, the brain is a sensing and interpreting organ. In much the same way that the eyes are receptive to light, and the ears to sound, the brain is receptive to thought energy. The brain is the thinking organ, just as the tongue is the tasting organ. The brain captures thought energy and allows it to take form in the mind as words, ideas, beliefs, paradigms, etc. The brain provides the physical structure for thought to exist.

One set of thought structures is called the ego. The ego is a set of thoughts that each of us uses to describe our selves. When I say, "I am a teacher," or, "I am 6 feet tall," or, "I am a good person," these thought descriptions of self are the ego. For us to function in the physical world, it is essential for each of us to discern a separation between our selves and the world around us. Using the gift of thought, we can describe the boundaries between us, other people, and objects in the environment.

Like any other thought patterns, it is helpful to remember that the divisions we discern are placed there by the thought process. Mind, brain and ego are simply words that describe processes and functions we experience. When we allow these words to become definitions - to define who we are - we misuse thought, and introduce dysfunction into our lives.

WELLNESS AND THE GIFT OF THOUGHT

Without the gift of thought, we would be unable to discern or describe our life experiences. Nor would we be capable of communicating with each other, for language is a powerful manifestation of this gift. We would be as plants: existing as life expressions and limited in awareness. Thought is a wondrous gift. Yet, we have already discussed how thought can be problematic as well. Difficulties arise when we misuse this gift.

We experience wellness with the gift of thought by using thought well, and avoiding the misuses outlined above. Here are a few tips:

➢ Remember that thought is a gift from a divine source. Thought does not originate in our minds; rather, thought comes into our minds from a source beyond. Be thankful for this gift.

➢ Make use of thought. This gift is given us to use, not to deny or ignore. The four "Ds" - discern, describe, design and decide - these are apt uses of thought. Avoid the misuses of thought - definition and judgment.

➢ Thought arises in the mind space, so keeping the mind open and spacious allows the thought processes to flow most naturally.

➢ The mind is anchored in the brain, which is an organ in the physical body. What's more, the brain is a living organ, sustained by the gift of life. Neural energy, the electrical impulses that occur in the brain and the nerves are elements of the life energy system. All of the points we made earlier - for wellness in the physical body and the life energy system - all are key to wellness of thought.

➢ Don't let thought define who you are. Thought creates useful boundaries. You are unlimited. You can describe your physical body in great detail, describe your life experiences, and even discuss thought itself with others. Yet, none of this defines who you are. Thought is a useful tool of awareness, but don't be limited by thought.

➢ Put the tool down. Just like any tool we would use, the gift of thought is not meant to be used all of the time. However, most of us have a continuous running commentary going in our minds – the thoughts never stop. For many, sleep is the only break from the thought stream. You can learn, however, to introduce pauses into the thought stream, by bringing awareness to your thoughts. Meditation and yoga practice are helpful ways of creating a quiet mind-space, and learning to pause the stream of thinking.

We experience well-being in the gift of thought, when our minds are clear and calm, and we are able to think succinctly and focus our thoughts. Stress, on the other hand, is the primary indicator of non-wellness in our thinking. When we experience stress, our thoughts are judging events, objects or people. Stress tells us that we are out of alignment in our thoughts. Of course, scientific research tells us that stress affects our bodies and life energy, too. Responding to stress is essential to well-being.

To reduce stress, we can follow the guidelines above for wellness in the gift of thought. The last point above – practicing yoga and meditation – is especially helpful for stress reduction.

CELEBRATING AND HONORING THE GIFT OF THOUGHT

Let's celebrate the gift of the thought. Here's an invocation I use each day.

*Thought is a gift of divine love
and I am grateful and honored to receive it.*

I commit this day:
    to strengthen and nurture this thought-gift, and
    to empower this mind-space with awareness

I allow all thought to come from a divine source

I offer all thought to divine service

I awaken to the divine intention of the universe

Divine spirit, make of me an open channel of love and grace, and let divine grace flow through me into this world.

Use me this day to create a sacred experience for all that I encounter.

Namaste

SPECIAL SECTION 2 - CREATION AND EVOLUTION

In the U.S. there has been a debate for years about the merits of teaching evolution and creation to school children. Much of this debate is fostered by a Christian polity, with an agenda that goes far beyond what's taught in school. Regardless of the source, this argument has created an either-or attitude, as if one must choose between these two ideas. Personally, I think this whole debate is silly. In my view, creation and evolution are both true, and both occur simultaneously at all times, everywhere in the universe.

Human history is filled with creation stories. Every culture, every tribe, every spiritual tradition has a creation story. These stories have a common thread – all teach us that humanity, and indeed, everything else, comes from a divine source. All of these stories contain an element of truth, and all are useful in helping us understand divine creation. (Any description we use for divine creation will, of course, be incomplete, since divine consciousness is beyond what we can comprehend and describe. Yet, the creation stories are helpful in our daily living.) The creation stories were not written to be history lessons, and one common mistake people make today is to interpret these stories literally.

Science, too, has a creation story. It is called "the big bang theory." Like all of the religious creation stories, this theory has its usefulness. The question of the source remains unanswered in the scientific story, because scientists choose not to address this issue.

All of these creation stories have one common flaw: creation is seen as a one-time event, and then the universe (and humans) move along from there. This "single event" idea of creation is clearly untrue. Look around you with an open heart and mind. The creative process is ongoing. We see it in the leaves on the trees, the sound of the wind, and the flowering of human awareness. Every moment is an expression of divine creation, coming into existence, and then, as with everything in this universe, passing away.

For me, creation is simply "the wave that rises up from the ocean." All things rise up in the field of consciousness and come into being, until such time as they fall away again. There is no permanence in the world of forms, only waves that come into existence for a while, then disassemble. The ocean is the infinite divine consciousness, the source of all. Each moment is one of continuous creation. Even our thoughts are waves that rise into the mind-space for a moment, before moving on.

Consciousness is the source of all creation, and the driving force for evolution. Evolution is one process by which creation occurs each moment. There has been great misunderstanding of evolution in western culture, because what we observe as evolution in species on this planet is only a small piece of the total picture. Evolution does not happen by accident, nor is evolution simply the result of survival instincts. Rather, evolution is driven by intention. Evolution is the process by which the universe grows in awareness.

If we examine the evolution of the universe, starting with the big bang, and using our own planet as an example, we can see that the early states of awareness were simply physical. Complex matter evolved from less complex structures. Structure is the expression of divine consciousness in physical matter, and more complex structure reflects greater awareness. As matter evolved, life became possible. Life first existed as simple organisms which were not much more than complex molecules. As life-awareness expanded, more complex organisms evolved from simpler ones. Eventually, some living organisms began to experience thought-awareness. Over time, thought has become the dominant level of awareness for humanity, and possibly for other species on this planet and elsewhere.

In the human species, evolution has been an expansion of awareness as well. The center of awareness of humanity has risen throughout history. There have always been some individuals who experienced more enlightened awareness than their peers, but these individuals have been rare. They have been the spiritual teachers, the avatars, the guides to spiritual awareness for the rest of us. The center of awareness for humanity as a whole, however, has expanded slowly over the many millennia of human existence.

Likewise, each individual grows in awareness throughout her lifetime. Each person evolves as an individual. The processes of human evolution and individual evolution occur simultaneously and in parallel - human awareness is the synergistic total of the awareness of individual persons.

Evolution does not always follow a straight-line, or a simple path. Sometimes a species may evolve rapidly via a large leap; other times, a species may perish because it is unable to evolve. Human evolution appears to be approaching a tipping point - a time when rapid change is likely, and there may be discomfort involved. Humanity has evolved to the point of thought-centered awareness. Western civilization, which now covers most of the world, is particularly thought-centered. Science, economics, medicine, government - all are thought-centered institutions. Over the past two hundred years or so, this thought-centered awareness has solved many problems humans face. Now, though, thought is also the source of most human dilemmas. It seems we have reached a point where our thinking creates as many problems as it solves, and we are stuck. Many problems seem intractable. Human thought has given us the tools to destroy ourselves, and the planet we live on. And humanity seems to be continuously repeating the same mistakes. Human thought has become the limiting factor in human evolution.

There is no stopping the evolutionary process, though. And human evolution is poised to make a step forward, with pure awareness, beyond thought, as the future center of human awareness. There are a growing number of individuals who are already aware of the limitations of our thinking, and when this number grows to a tipping point, a shift will occur. There will be resistance to this shift, and some people won't make it. Many human institutions - those that are built on thought foundations - will perish. Yet, humanity as a whole will come to understand thought as a gift of divine love, a useful, and limited, tool for understanding. Human awareness will continue to expand.

DIVINE PLAY

There is a word in Sanskrit - *leila* - which means "divine play." The spirit of *leila* is that the divine universe is creating and evolving in a playful game of self-expression. The un-manifest becomes manifest in an infinite number of creative acts, and the manifest becomes aware of the un-manifest. This playful game of hide and seek is divine consciousness becoming aware of itself through its creations.

We are invited to play hide-and-seek with God. Our existence, our experience, everything that we receive, think and do, is a part of this divine play. The intent of the divine source is to create awareness, and to experience joy. Games are meant to be fun! That's why I don't engage in arguments about creation and evolution, or about spiritual ideas. To argue about something that is intended to be fun is just absurd. It is like a group of kids arguing over whether a batted ball is fair or foul, instead of playing the game.

We are not capable of fully understanding the divine. Yet, we know that the universe is *leila*. We're not supposed to take everything so seriously.

So, let yourself play.

Chapter 4
THE GIFT OF AWARENESS

*"At the heart of the new
consciousness
lies the
transcendence
of thought,
the new-found
ability of rising
above thought,
of realizing
a dimension
within your-
self that is
infinitely
more vast
than
thought"*

*- Eckhardt
Tolle*

The Gift of Awareness

Summary

Consciousness expressed as	Pure awareness
Kosha	Vijnana Maya Kosha – the layer of understanding, beyond the mind
Level of Consciousness	0 to 999
Intention	Being Guiding our use of the other gifts Awakening to the Divine Presence
Manifestation of dis-ease	Non-peace
Key to wellness	Peace, Joy, Love

Awareness is a gift of divine love, and I am grateful and honored to receive it. Through this gift of awareness, I am able to be, and to observe and guide my use of all of the gifts I have received.

I find it challenging to describe the gift of awareness in words. Language is an expression of thought; awareness expands beyond the limits of thought. So, any words used to describe the gift of awareness will be too limited. Nevertheless, I believe this gift is the most important concept in you can grasp in this book. Why? Because this gift of awareness, which is beyond the limits of thought, is the future of humanity. Through expanded, transcendent awareness, each of us, and humanity as a whole, will survive and thrive.

Although words are too limited to describe the gift of awareness, some words are useful. The words used by the ancient sages of India were *Vishnana Maya Kosha*, or the layer of understanding and wisdom. In this context, understanding is more than just the sum of the knowledge and thinking we have. Wisdom recognizes both the power, and the limitations of thought.

Other words may also be used: spiritual awareness, the soul, pure awareness, transcendent awareness, the *atman*, awakened awareness, enlightened awareness, pure being. All of these words point to the same truth – that we are capable of awareness that expands beyond the limits of thought. And, that through this expanded awareness, we are able to gain wisdom and understanding that is impossible to know with thought alone.

The gift of awareness surrounds, permeates and guides all of the previous three gifts – the gift of physical body, the gift of life, and the gift of thought. And the gift of awareness expands beyond these others, into the realm of being. This gift lacks a form that can be fully described in words. It is simply the experience of "I am".

On Dr. David Hawkin's map of consciousness, the gift of awareness covers the entire range, from 0 to 1,000. At the lower numbers, awareness resonates with the physical world, and we experience the gift of the physical body. As awareness expands to the higher numbers (on the map) we experience the gift of life, and the gift of thought. Beyond the limits of thought, we experience pure awareness, the true essence of our being.

To fully understand and experience awareness, we move beyond the limits of words, beyond the limits of thought. We awaken to a new way of being. This awakening, this flowering of awareness is the next step in human evolution. The center of gravity of human awareness has for many years existed at the level of thought. We seem to be stuck in our minds. When we awaken to the gift of awareness, beyond thought, all of the limits placed on our selves by our minds simply fall away, and we become the expansive, joyful beings we were meant to be.

Awakening to the gift of pure awareness offers us a holistic perspective on ourselves. We become aware that the five gifts are not separate from each other, but simply unique expressions of divine grace. While recognizing the usefulness of the models we use to describe the body, life and thought, we know that these are only tools of thought. We awaken to the truth of the divine source of all the gifts we've received.

The gift of pure awareness is also the source of meaningful relationships. Relationships require *being* together, in present moment awareness. Only by moving beyond the limits of thought do we see the divine light we share with other people.

Through awareness, we witness ourselves and the world we live in with greater clarity. We view the body as a structured collection of matter that we share with the structures and objects in the environment. Life is seen as a loving, living energy system that is shared with all living beings. Thought is a gift, and each thought enters the mind space from a place beyond our comprehension. And all comes from a divine source.

INTENTION AND THE GIFT OF AWARENESS

Can we truly know the intention of the divine universe, or our reason for being in it? I'm not sure. What I do know, however, is that the universe is a field of intention, and everything in it happens for a purpose. This includes our being here. In fact, this understanding points to the intention of the gift of awareness – simply being.

It is through the gift of awareness that we come to be in the world, and to be aware of our existence. This is the gift that knows "I am." Sometimes this is referred to as the witness – the awareness that witnesses all that happens within each of us. We can think of this gift as a field of awareness, within which arises all that we think, experience and do. To know this awareness, we need simply to be.

The gift of awareness is also intended to be the guide for the other gifts. Through this gift, we can be aware of, and guide our thoughts. With awareness and thought, we can guide and understand our life experiences, and choose the actions we take with our bodies. Guidance begins with awareness.

Additionally, it is through the gift of awareness that we can know the divine source. This is our awakening. Our normal view is of the manifest world – we tend to focus on what we think, experience and do in the world. We have a camera that only looks inward, to the world and our role in it. Through expanded awareness, we can turn the camera around, and see our place as an expression of divine consciousness. Awakening, through the gift of awareness, we can view the source of all that is manifest.

WELLNESS AND THE GIFT OF AWARENESS

Of all the gifts we receive, awareness is the most powerful and the most subtle. It is also the wellspring of holistic wellness. It is this gift that allows us to see the truth, to experience love and connectedness, and to receive divine grace. Wellness flows from pure awareness.

All that we discussed earlier about wellness in the first three gifts applies here as well. It is difficult to remain aware when the physical body is in pain, or the life energy is weak, or the mind is disturbed. Through awareness, we come to know that there are no separations between the gifts, and that wellness must be a holistic endeavor.

The key to wellness, then, is to be aware. Bring awareness to all that you are, all that you think, all that you experience, and all that you do. And be aware of the divine source of all things.

CELEBRATING AND HONORING THE GIFT OF AWARENESS

Let's celebrate the gift of the awareness. Here's an invocation I use each day.

Awareness is a gift of divine love
and I am grateful and honored to receive it.

I commit this day:
        To grow in awareness, and
        To guide all that I think, all that I experience and all
        that I do with awareness.

I offer this entire being to divine service.

I awaken to the divine consciousness of the universe.

Divine spirit, make of me an open channel of love and grace,
and let divine grace flow through me into this world.

Use me this day to create a sacred experience for all that I
encounter.

Namaste

Chapter 5
THE GIFT OF DIVINE GRACE

*"Every flower has
its own colour
but every
colour comes
from the
same light."*

*- Sri
Nisargadatta
Maharishi*

The universe is a manifestation of divine consciousness, and this divine presence is in all things all the time. I am grateful and honored to be in the presence of the divine. When I am open to the divine presence, I experience the gift of divine grace, and my whole world is illumined by this gift. This is the source of all gifts I receive, and of all that I am, all that I think, all that I experience, and all that I do. Everything comes from a divine, loving source.

More than any other part of this book, I have struggled with the words to describe this gift. Language is incapable of fully capturing this truth. I have considered many, equally true ways of describing this gift:

> *The Gift of Divine Love*
> *The Gift of Divine Light*
> *The Gift of Divine Joy*
> *The Gift of Oneness*

Any of these choices can help point us in the right direction, towards awakening. Many other words can be helpful, too. The divine source is the great mystery that is described in all spiritual and religious traditions, though each describes the divine in its own way. In the ancient teachings of the *Maya Koshas*, this gift is called *Ananda Maya Kosha*, or the layer of bliss. Here we have a description, not of what it the divine source is, but of what we experience when we become aware it. We experience bliss.

Divine consciousness is a property of the universe. Indeed, it is the one unchanging, unchangeable, fundamental property. Consciousness is the source of all that is manifest. Yet, consciousness itself is un-manifest. The divine is the source of all forms, yet is formless itself. It is infinite, unbounded and beyond comprehension.

The process by which we become aware of the divine source is called *awakening*. Implied in this description is the idea that we are asleep, that the person who is unaware of the divine source is unconscious of the truth. When one is awakened, one experiences the light, love, joy and bliss of the divine source.

It is possible to experience an "awakened state", which is a temporary realization of oneness with the divine source. Many people, myself included, have had such experiences. As we grow in awareness, these experiences become more frequent and more prolonged. A person who is fully awakened experiences oneness with all that is, all the time.

There is nothing we can do to force ourselves through the awakening process. Oh, the small egoic mind does not like this statement. In our culture, we are taught that we must be spiritual seekers, and that with effort and will we can move ourselves into awakening. Sorry, but it is not true. Awakening comes from the divine. We can open to the process, but we can not make it happen.

What we can do, is make room for the awakening to occur. Through our spiritual practice, we can grow in awareness beyond the limits of thought. We can quiet the mind, and experience the gift of divine grace. We can experience awakened states of awareness, where we know the love and grace of the divine source. And, we can allow the process to unfold.

Spiritual teachings can also help us experience the divine source, when the writings are understood as metaphors for truth. Poetry and spiritual literature are filled with metaphor as a way of guiding us toward our higher self. These metaphors help us understand the unlimited nature of divine consciousness.

For me, the most helpful metaphor is to think of the divine source as a vast ocean. Each of us is a wave that rises up on the ocean. We are transient waves, moving through the manifest world. Still, the vast infinite ocean is within each of us, supporting us with love and grace in all that we do.

Ultimately, to truly know the divine, we need to let go of the limits of thought, and allow the gift of divine grace to come to us. This is the surrender that has been talked about in all religions. We can not force the universe, we can only allow it to manifest. And when it does, we experience "the peace that passeth all understanding," as the Bible puts it. We experience all of the wonderful gifts we've been given, and more. We experience our true self, which is divine consciousness become manifest.

SPECIAL SECTION 3 – The Big Question

In his most recent book, The Grand Design, mathematician and physicist Dr. Steven Hawking claims that we do not need God to explain the creation of the universe (12). Such a statement is guaranteed to grab headlines. But, is it true?

While the media and many religious leaders react with vigor to such a statement, I tend to take a different view. To me, *explanation* is something we do with our thinking. As we discussed in chapter 4, the gift of thought is both powerful and limited, at the same time. Explanation, as a function of thought, is governed by the power and the limits of thought. In other words, our ability to explain things is equivalent to our ability to think. What's more, anything that can be explained lies within these same limits. We can only explain that which is explainable. We cannot use thought to grasp that which is beyond thought.

When I reflect on the question of divine involvement in the creation of the universe (or anything else, for that matter), I find myself drawn to and asking a bigger question:

Does God exist?

When we ask this question, we move very quickly into sticky territory, for many reasons. First, we need to keep in mind that the word "God" is just a word. This word, which is an English word, might not have any meaning to someone for whom English is not a native tongue. What's more, in English, and especially in the culture of the United States, the word "God" usually refers to a Christian concept. Since this is the cultural and religious tradition of my birth, the word "God" comes easily to me. Yet, I could just as accurately ask,

Does Allah exist? or,
Does Yahweh exist? or,
Does Brahma exist? or,
Does the Tao exist?

Or, any number of questions, which, in different cultural and religious contexts, have equivalent meaning. We can change the wording and language, to help clarify and universalize the question, but that does not bring us closer to an answer.

In the context of the five gifts, I would ask this question thus: *Is there a divine source to all that is?*

This question has challenged the greatest of human minds throughout history. Mountains of volumes have been written by many people, in an attempt to answer this question. The arguments pro and con are equally formidable and voluminous. And yet, the question remains. Why?

Because, no amount of argument or debate can answer this question. Argument, debate, writing, language, words - all of these are tools of the gift of thought. Thought is a powerful gift; and a limited one. Some questions are easily answered within the limits of this gift, and some concepts are well described by words. When we try to answer spiritual questions, however, thought falls short. Questions of divine presence or intent require awareness far beyond the limits of thought. No words can fully describe or explain the divine, because the gift of thought, powerful though it is, is not conscious enough to encompass the divine. The best we can do with thought is use words, like "God" to point to an awareness beyond words.

Of course, human awareness expands beyond the limits of thought, and through the gift of awareness we can glimpse the truth of divine presence. Historically, only a small number of people have been at this expanded level of awareness. We have called these individuals sages, spiritual teachers, enlightened ones. Doesn't it make sense to ask this question to the most aware, most enlightened people? What answer have the most enlightened sages given, throughout history, when asked the question, does God exist? Simply:

Yes.

In the past, only a small number of people have been aware enough to experience the gift of divine grace. That's changing. There is an evolutionary shift in human awareness underway, and a growing number of individuals have awakened to awareness that transcends the limits of thought. Spiritual awareness is available to all of us. With practice, each of us can answer the question of divine presence through a knowing that can't be put into words, yet is more clear than any idea that can be spoken.

You have this capacity for awareness, too. Begin your practice by bringing your awareness to your thoughts. As you go through your day, notice how thought emerges in your mindspace. And become aware of your awareness - that part of your awareness that observes your thinking - that is awareness that transcends thought. With practice, this awareness becomes more palpable, and you begin to know, to experience, to be immersed in the blissful infinite joy of the Divine Presence.

When you experience the gift of awareness beyond thought, you will no longer need to argue the truth of divine presence. Nor will you need faith, belief, or any other process to answer this question for you. You will simply know.

Chapter 6
BONUS GIFT: THE GIFT OF WELL-BEING

The conscious universe is a loving, divine presence. Each of the five gifts is an expression of divine grace, given to us with no limits or demands attached. Inherent in the gifts we receive is the intention that we have joy and wellness in our experience.

Each of us has within us the capacity for being well. Well-being is experienced when we remember the true nature of our selves and the world around us. Forgetfulness, or ignorance, leads to *dis-ease*, a lack of joy, and an imbalance in our lives.

Each of the five gifts also has a means of reminding us - just in case we forget. If we ignore the signals, our ignorance and forgetfulness grows, and our wellness declines. Recognizing and responding to an experience of imbalance, and allowing ourselves to be reminded, is the key to restoring well-being. Using an understanding of the five gifts, then, here are six steps to well-being.

> **Remember the divine source**. Divine consciousness is beyond what our words can describe. Yet, we can remember that this is our source, and the source of all things. When we forget our source, we feel separated from love and grace, and from each other. Detachment and loneliness dominate our experience. When we remember the divine source, and know that it is within us at all times, and we open ourselves to the gift of divine grace.

> **Know yourself to be a manifestation of the divine source**. You are the wave that rises up on the ocean, and the ocean is within you. Let yourself be the wave of awareness. As Louise Hay said, "I am not a human being having an occasional spiritual experience, I am a spiritual being having a human experience."(5) Let yourself

be what you truly are - pure awareness. Allow others to be divine manifestations as well. And allow all that you think, experience and do be guided by the gift of awareness.

> **Let thought be a tool of awareness**. As we said earlier, many people are thought-centered in their awareness, and most are not connected with awareness beyond thought in their daily living. Yet, when you remember that you are the awareness behind the thought, the field within which the thought arises, you can use the gift of thought as a tool for awareness. When we forget the source of thought - which is divine - we let thinking control our lives. Stress becomes the dominant experience. Stress is the main source of poor health in western culture because this culture is so thought-centric. To relieve stress, we simply need to remember who we really are - the field of awareness within which the thought arises. Let yourself use the gift of thought well, without being consumed by your thinking.

> **Move and flow with living energy**. Remember that life is a divine gift, one which we share with all living things. Let the *prana* - the life energy - flow to you, within you, and through you. Allow yourself to be moved with life, and to flow with the stream. Stiffness, strain and negative emotions are all signs that the life flow is blocked or restricted. Motion and joyful emotion allow the energy system to be a vital expression of divine grace. Let yourself be moved by the gift of life.

> **Nurture the physical body, and let it go**. Remember that the physical body is a gift, and all of the "stuff" that makes up the physical body comes from the world around us. We nurture the body by giving it healthy nutrition and a healthy environment, from which the body re-

juvenates itself. At the same time, we must let the body go, letting each molecule and each atom be what it is – a gift from the divine. Pain is a signal that we are out of alignment with the needs of the body. Bringing awareness to the body, and letting go of what is out of alignment with the divine source, is the key to relieving pain. We experience well-being when we align the gift of the physical body with the design that comes from the divine source.

> **Most importantly, be whole, be one**. Throughout this book, we've been talking about the five gifts, and how each is a unique manifestation of the divine source. It is very easy to forget that this is a thought-model only. In words there are separations; in truth, there is only oneness. You are a whole being, a holy being, inseparable from the divine source, filled with divine consciousness and love. There is no separation between yourself and the chair you are sitting on, or the animals and plants in the world around you, or any other person, or even a star in a galaxy billions of light years away. You are one with all that is, and with the divine source of all that is.

There is one consciousness, and you are its manifestation in this world. Use the five gifts to promote oneness and you will experience the joyful well-being that is intended for you.

Epilogue – We are Ready to Evolve

We are ready to evolve.

We have reached a point where thinking, which has served humanity so well for thousands of years, is now creating as many problems as it solves. Where we can create a stack of books, as high as the mountains, filled with logical thoughts supporting one side of an issue, and an equally high, equally logical stack supporting the other side, and the debate gets us no closer to resolving the issue. Where great institutions, based entirely on scientific research (a set of ideas), like western medicine, now cause as much harm as good. (Did you know that the number three cause of death in the USA is western medicine?) Where governments and organizations based on the rule of law (another set of ideas) have become mostly dysfunctional, unable to meet the needs of their people or resolve the issues they face. (In the US, Congress changes from one party to the other every two years, and is gridlocked during the time in between, unable to function in any meaningful way.)

We are ready to evolve.

We have reached a point where our thinking can destroy us, as easily as it can save us. We are fully capable of thinking our way into self-destruction. Are we capable of thinking our way out of it?

We are ready to evolve.

We have reached a point where every major religion based on a set of beliefs (thoughts) has internal factions that use their beliefs to justify killing and destroying. Where the spiritual messages of the great teachers on whom these religions are founded have been lost in a jumble of dogmas (thoughts) and rules (more thoughts) that serve the religious hierarchy, but little else. Where religion is used to justify harm as often as for healing.

We are ready to evolve.

We, humanity, are ready to grow beyond the limits of our thinking. Thought, which has empowered human evolution for ten millennia, no longer serves us in this way. We have reached a glass ceiling, were our thinking limits our evolution.

We are ready to evolve beyond these limits. This does not mean that we will abandon thought. Rather, we are ready to grow in awareness, to be aware of both the way that thinking serves us, and how it limits us.

We are ready to experience an expanded, spiritual awareness. Through this awareness, we will guide our thoughts, our experiences, and our actions, to create a better world for humanity, and for all life.

In the past, such expanded awareness was accessible to just a few individuals. We called these people enlightened, Buddha, Christ, saints and sages. Now, the gift of awareness is offered to us all. We are all ready to evolve.

As Dr. David Hawkins says, homo erectus evolved into homo sapiens, and now we are ready to grow, to become homo spiritus (4). This step in evolution requires us each to evolve personally - and for us to evolve together in community, in humanity.   We are ready! Will you join us?

Namaste
Joe

Notes and References

All of the graphics and pictures used in this book are public domain, or created by the author, unless otherwise noted below.

1. The quote on page 4, "I am a hole. . ." is by the Sufi poet Hafiz, translated into English by Daniel Ladinsky in The Gift, 1999
2. Two sources on the Maya Koshas.
   a. The Yoga Tradition, by Georg Feuerstein, PhD., Hohm Press, 2001. p. 350
   b. The Upanishads, Breath of the Eternal, translated from Sanskrit by Swami Prabhavananda and Frederick Manchester, 1975, Mentor Books
3. Integral Vision, by Ken Wilbur, Shambala Publications, Inc., 2007, p. 115-116. Ken Wilber is one of the most brilliant teachers of this era.
4. Power Vs. Force, by Dr. David Hawkins, (Veritas Publishing, 2002), The Eye of the I (Veritas Publishing, 2001), and other sources, including Dr. Hawkins' radio programs and recordings. I consider Dr. Hawkins' to be one of my most important spiritual teachers. The graphics, interpretations and descriptions of his works in this book are mine. The calibrations in this book using The Map of Consciousness are also done by me, and have not been reviewed or endorsed by Dr. Hawkins.
5. The quote on page 14, "We shape clay. . ." by Lao-Tsu is from Tao Te Ching, translated by Stephen Mitchell, Harper Collins Publishers, 1988, p. 11
6. The photo of the human skeleton on page 17 is by Mikael Hagstrom, used under the GNU free documentation license. The photo of DNA on page 17 is by Tim Vickers, used under the GNU free documentation license. The image of cells on page 17 is by John Schmidt, used under the GNU free documentation license.

7. The quote on page 26, "my limbs are. . ." by Rabindranath Tagore, is from <u>Singing in the Living Tradition</u>, Unitarian Universalist Association Press, 1993, #529

8. <u>Anatomy Trains, Myofascial Meridians for Manual and Movement Therapists</u>, by Thomas W. Myers, 2nd Edition, Churchill Livingstone, 2008

9. The quote on page 34, "the mind does not. . ." by Deepak Chopra is from the audio program *Living Beyond Miracles*, by Wayne Dyer and Deepak Chopra, New World Library, 2005

10. The quote on page 54, "At the heart. . ." by Eckhart Tolle is from <u>A New Earth, Awakening to Your Life's Purpose</u>, page 21, published by Namaste Publishing, 2005

11. The quote on page 62, "Every flower has. . ." is by Sri Nisargadatta Maharishi, from <u>I am That: Talks with Sri Nisargadatta Maharishi</u>, Acorn Press, 1990

12. <u>The Grand Design</u>, by Stephen Hawking and Leonard Mlodinow, Bantam Publishing, 2010

About the Author

In the last ten years, Joe Hahn, RYT, has helped thousands of people grow in awareness, through his teaching of yoga and meditation, and his writings. Joe has made an extensive study of world religions, with a focus on the traditions of India, where yoga originates. In his writing and teaching, he combines ancient wisdom and modern spiritual thinking. His spiritual philosophy is simple: *each of us is a unique, beautiful expression of the divine, and we all share the same divine light.* This idea underpins all of his teaching and writing.

Joe has studied extensively with John Friend, creator of Anusara Yoga, and his yoga teaching is strongly influenced by Anusara Yoga. Additionally, Joe has studied the works of many contemporary spiritual teachers, including Dr. David Hawkins, Eckhardt Tolle, Ken Wilbur, Dr. Wayne Dwyer, Dr. Deepak Chopra, Louise Hay, and many others.

Joe is a registered yoga teacher with the Yoga Alliance, a certified hatha yoga instructor, and a certified Oneness Blessing (Deeksha) giver. He teaches weekly yoga classes, and offers meditation and oneness blessings each week. Joe lives with his family near Baltimore, Maryland.

Learn more about Joe's writings and teaching at:

www.the5gifts.com.